SHARKS!

PHONICS

Shark Teeth

Book 5: th (Beginning and Ending)

By Quinlan B. Lee

Photo Credits: cover: Mike Parry/Minden Pictures; title page: David Jenkins/Getty Images; page 2: Joel Sartore/National Geographic/Getty Images; page 4: Mike Parry/Minden Pictures; page 6: James Watt/Getty Images; pages 8-9: Daoart/Shutterstock; page 10: David Jenkins/Getty Images; page 12: Antonio Busiello; pages 14-15: George Karbus Photography/Corbis; page 16: Image Source/Getty Images.

ISBN 978-0-545-74703-5

12 11 10 9 8 7 6 5 4 3 2 1   14 15 16 17 18/0

Printed in China   145

First Printing, September 2014

SCHOLASTIC INC.

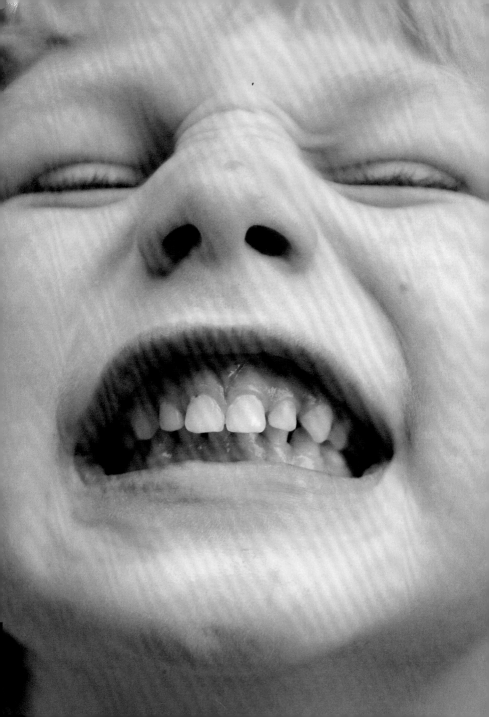

Look in your **mouth**.

How many **teeth** do you have?

Do you have ten **teeth**?

Do you have twenty **teeth**?

Do you have a spot where a **tooth** is missing?

People have **thirty**-two **teeth** when **they** grow up.

How many **teeth** do you **think** sharks have?

Do you **think** sharks have **thirty teeth**?

Do you **think they** have forty **teeth**?

If you look in a shark's **mouth**, you will see five rows of **teeth**. Some sharks have a hundred **teeth**. Some sharks have **three thousand teeth**!

Usually people lose **their** first baby **tooth** around **their** **sixth** birthday.

Sharks lose **teeth** all **the** time.

They are always growing new **teeth**.
In a shark's life, it can grow **thirty thousand teeth**!

Sharks catch all sorts of **things** with **their teeth**.

These things go in **through their mouths**.

Then they go into **their** stomachs.

What **things** do you **think** you would find in a shark's stomach?

Did you **think** you would find fish?

Did you **think** you would find cows?

Did you **think** you would find hippos?

You would be right!

Even elephant parts have been found in sharks.

Other **things** have been found in sharks, too.
Things like paint cans, bikes, coats, and lots of **cloth** have been found in sharks.

Shark **teeth** can chew almost anything!